MARTIN LUTHER KING JR.

and the March Toward Freedom

by Rita Hakim

Gateway Civil Rights
The Millbrook Press
Brookfield, Connecticut

Photographs courtesy of: AP/Wide World Photos: cover, 2-3,
4, 10, 12, 13, 15, 20, 22-23, 25, 27, 29, 30; The Bettmann
Archive: cover inset, 1, 22; Schomburg Center for Research in
Black Culture: 6; Washington Post/D.C. Public Library: 9, 17;
District of Columbia Public Library: 19.

Cataloging-in-Publication Data

Hakim, Rita.
Martin Luther King, Jr., and the march toward freedom.

32 p.; ill.: (Gateway Civil Rights)
Bibliography: p.
Includes index.

Summary: A biography of the U.S. civil rights leader Martin
Luther King, Jr., describing his role in the struggle of
blacks for equality in the 1950s and 1960s.

1. King, Martin Luther, Jr., 1929-1968.
2. Civil rights movements—United States—
History—20th century.
3. United States—Race relations.
B 1991
ISBN 1-878841-13-0

Martin Luther King, Jr., led thousands of marchers through Chicago in 1966 to protest racial prejudice in the city.

Movements are born when many people share a belief that things must change. But every great movement needs a leader. Often, it takes a single person to shape a clear vision of how the world can be.

In the 1960s, a great movement swept the United States. People around the nation realized that society did not treat all of its citizens fairly. They got together to demand equal rights for all.

The basic rights of citizens are called civil rights. In the 1960s, black Americans led the fight for civil rights. Many people had different ideas about how to win these rights. But one man came forward to lead them. His name was Martin Luther King, Jr. His most famous speech was titled "I Have a Dream." His dream was the dream of everyone involved in the civil rights movement: peace, justice, and equality.

Martin was a tireless worker for civil rights.

First Prize

Martin Luther King, Jr., grew up in Atlanta, Georgia. He lived in a rambling house with his mother, father, sister, brother, grandmother, and grandfather. The King family was very close, and the household was active. The King children took piano lessons, played sports, and did odd jobs.

Martin's mother, Alberta, was in charge of music lessons. His father, Martin Luther King, Sr. (also known as Daddy King), was a Baptist minister. He was in charge of the children's religious and moral education.

Daddy King was a serious, intelligent man. He believed in justice, even though black people in the South were treated poorly by white society. If a black family wanted to go to a restaurant, they had to sit in a separate section. If they wanted to see a movie, they had to sit way in the back of the

The King family. Daddy King is standing in the center. The arrow shows Martin seated to the right.

balcony. Blacks even had to use separate public water fountains marked "For Colored Only."

Once Daddy King took Martin to buy some shoes. The clerk made them go to the back of the store. "We don't serve colored in the front of the store," he told them.

Daddy King was filled with anger, but he did not show it. "If you don't serve colored in the front of the store, then you don't serve these colored at all!" he told the clerk. He took Martin by the hand and left the store.

Martin learned dignity from both his parents. White people might be cruel to him, but he would not show anger or hatred. His mother told him, "You're as good as anyone." And he believed it.

Martin was the best student in his class. By the time he was 14 years old, he seemed to be taking after his father. He liked his studies, and he liked speaking in public. Daddy King thought Martin might make a good minister.

That year, Martin and his speech teacher, Mrs. Sarah Bradley, traveled across the state to a competition. Martin gave a speech called "The Negro and the Constitution." The judges were surprised that this 14-year-old boy spoke so well and so seriously. Martin had thought deeply about the rights of blacks. The judges awarded him first prize.

Mrs. Bradley was overjoyed, and Martin was proud of himself. They boarded the bus to go back to Atlanta, but soon there was a problem. Some white people boarded the bus, and the driver told

Mrs. Bradley and Martin to move so that the whites could have their seats. Mrs. Bradley got up. There were laws in the South that kept blacks separate from whites. These were called Jim Crow laws. One of these laws said that blacks had to give up bus and train seats to whites.

Martin did not want to give up his seat, but Mrs. Bradley made him do it. Afterward, he burned with anger and shame. He had just given a speech about the rights that blacks have as citizens of the United States. Now, he was being denied one of those rights.

"That night will never leave my memory," he said later. "It was the angriest I have ever been in my life."

Martin thought a great deal about that bus ride. He became angry at all white people. They had set up a system that kept blacks poor. Blacks had no chance to get ahead when the laws were against them.

College

Martin wanted to do something about the unfair laws, but for now all he could do was continue his studies. He finished high school when he was just 15 years old. He went on to Morehouse College in Atlanta, where he continued to be a serious student. There, he decided once and for all that he wanted to be a minister. He made up his mind to attend another school, the Crozer Theological Seminary, to continue his religious education.

Crozer was in Pennsylvania, where there were no Jim Crow laws. Blacks had more freedom. Still, there were very few black students in the school. Some people thought blacks were lazy and stupid, but Martin proved them wrong. He always wore a neat suit and tie. He studied hard and asked intelligent questions. He was a model student.

Martin attended Morehouse College from 1944 to 1948.

At Crozer, Martin read many books that influenced his thinking. The most important was a book about Mohandas Gandhi, the great leader from India. Gandhi believed in using love, not hate, in the struggle against India's enemies. The Bible said the same thing. Martin decided that this was the only way blacks could get justice in the United States.

Martin was the top student in his class at Crozer. Afterward, he went on to Boston University. There he met a smart and attractive young woman named Coretta Scott. Coretta was studying music. Martin liked her right from the start and asked her out on a date. On their first date, Martin announced that he wanted to marry her. Coretta was shocked, but she soon learned to love this serious, determined man.

Mohandas Gandhi

A tiny, smiling man who wore a simple white robe—that was Mohandas Gandhi. He carried no weapons and commanded no army. Yet he forced the great British Empire out of India.

Gandhi knew that the British Empire was powerful. Indians could not fight the British with guns. But Gandhi had another plan. He organized Indians and told them not to obey laws that were unfair. He also told them not to fight back. His method was known as nonviolent resistance.

Indians followed his lead. They organized strikes and protests around the country. This created many problems for the British. Many Indians were arrested, but they did not fight. Instead, they simply filled the jails.

Gandhi led the peaceful protests. The English laughed at this little man with his calm, peaceful ways. But in 1947, they were forced to grant India its independence. Mohandas Gandhi had helped bring it about. His idea of nonviolent resistance had won, as he had said it would. Martin Luther King, Jr., believed that this same idea would work for black Americans.

Mohandas Gandhi worked for justice in India and inspired millions of people around the world.

The Minister and the Boycott

Martin and Coretta were married in the summer of 1953. They moved back to the South the following year. Martin had received an offer to be a minister in Montgomery, Alabama, at the Dexter Avenue Baptist Church.

Martin began his first preaching job in 1954. That was an important year for blacks. The Supreme Court of the United States ruled in 1954 that schools could not be segregated, or divided, by race. Until then, black children and white children in the South went to separate schools, and the schools for blacks were never as good. The Supreme Court changed that in one ruling. It was the beginning of a time of hope for blacks.

Martin Luther King, Jr., felt that things were changing in Montgomery. Blacks were talking about what they could do to make society more equal.

On December 1, 1955, a black woman named Rosa Parks took the first step. She refused to give up her seat on a bus to a white man. She was arrested.

Rosa contacted E. D. Nixon. He was the head of the Alabama branch of the National Association for the Advancement of Colored People, the NAACP. Then E. D. Nixon called Martin Luther King, Jr. The two men wanted to help Rosa Parks fight the unfair law.

Rosa Parks went to court to fight segregation on city buses.

Together with a group called the Women's Political Council, they organized a boycott of the Montgomery buses. In a boycott, people stop buying a product or using a service. It is a way to protest. The black leaders in Montgomery hoped the boycott would hurt the bus company's income.

Martin and the other black ministers in Montgomery preached to their congregations about the boycott. They explained the situation and asked people not to ride the buses. But Martin was worried. He knew that most blacks did not have cars. They depended on the buses to get to work.

On the day of the boycott, however, almost every black in town stopped riding the buses. They walked, or got lifts, or rode on mules or horses. The boycott was working.

But the trouble was not over. The bus company did not want to change its rules, and the city did not want to make the laws fair for blacks. So the ministers asked the people to continue the boycott. For over a year, Montgomery's blacks boycotted the buses. Martin Luther King, Jr., was now known to be the leader of the protest. He and Coretta received angry phone calls. People threatened to harm their baby daughter, Yolanda. Once, their house was bombed. No one was hurt, but Martin now knew that his life was in danger.

Coretta and her children packed food to bring to Martin in prison. He was often jailed for fighting segregation.

Still, the boycott continued. At last, in November 1956, the Supreme Court ruled on the matter. The Court decided that Montgomery's bus segregation law was wrong. It went against the U.S. Constitution, which guarantees people certain rights. Montgomery's blacks had won a major victory. Martin Luther King, Jr., appeared on the cover of *Time* magazine. He had become famous.

The Movement

Now a new spirit was sweeping across the South. Blacks felt they could change the bad old ways. And the leader of that movement was Martin Luther King, Jr. In 1957, Martin called together black leaders from all around the country. Together they formed a new group to fight for black civil rights: the Southern Christian Leadership Conference, or SCLC. Martin Luther King, Jr., was made its president.

Martin was very busy now. He was attending meetings, writing sermons, and preaching to his congregation. But he still found time to write a book about the Montgomery bus boycott called *Stride Toward Freedom*.

One day Martin was in New York signing copies of his book. Many admirers were crowded around, hoping to say a few words to the dignified, calm man who was leading the fight for justice. Suddenly a mentally ill black woman stepped forward and stabbed him in the chest with a letter opener. Martin stared at the woman in shock. Then he was rushed to the hospital.

He recovered from the wound, but not from the surprise. He did not understand why the woman would want to kill him. Still, he asked that she be put in a hospital, not a prison. He still believed in using love against his enemies.

Martin needed Coretta's support during the Montgomery bus boycott.

A few months later, Martin and Coretta traveled to India. Martin wanted to visit the land of Mohandas Gandhi. He and Coretta saw the poverty of India and understood that Gandhi had faced problems at least as large as their own.

Back home, the SCLC was busy organizing marches and demonstrations. Martin was needed to lead them. He decided to give up his job as pastor of the Dexter Avenue Baptist Church and join his father as co-pastor of Ebenezer Baptist Church in Atlanta. In his last sermon at Dexter Avenue, he asked his congregation to keep fighting until ''every black boy and girl can walk the streets with dignity and honor.'' The people were sorry to see him go, but they knew he was needed around the country.

Other people in the South were now using Martin's idea of nonviolence. In 1960 in Greensboro, North Carolina, for instance, four black students sat down at a lunch counter. The counter was for whites only. Whites hollered at the students, but they stayed put. The students were pushed and beaten, but they peacefully protested the unfair law.

Other "sit-ins" took place all over the South. In some places, people marched in the streets to protest unfair Jim Crow laws. Television was full of news stories about the civil rights movement that was growing in the South. In most places, the protesters followed Martin Luther King, Jr.'s teachings of nonviolence. The protests were peaceful, and that made them even more effective.

Birmingham

Martin was now a national leader. From his base in Atlanta, he traveled around the country, helping to organize demonstrations. He was arrested many times. He and Coretta now had four children: Yolanda, Martin Luther III, Dexter, and Bernice. The children were used to seeing pictures of their father being arrested by the police. Coretta taught them that their father had done nothing wrong. It was the laws that were wrong, and he was showing that to the country.

In 1963, the SCLC went to Birmingham, Alabama. Birmingham was known as one of the worst cities in the South for blacks. Martin and the other leaders felt they were ready to take on Birmingham.

Martin with Ralph Abernathy on the steps of the Lincoln Memorial in Washington.

Martin spoke to the city's leaders. He demanded that they strike down the laws that kept public places segregated. Many of the city's stores had signs that said ''whites only.'' But Birmingham's leaders refused to change things.

So the SCLC organized the town's blacks. Demonstrations were held at ''whites only'' stores. Martin gave speeches in black churches. Many people were afraid to protest because they were afraid of going to jail. But Martin told them they were fighting for freedom. ''If the road to freedom leads through the jailhouse,'' he said, ''then, turnkey, swing wide the gates!'' After every speech, more and more blacks joined the protests.

On April 12, 1963, Martin led a march through the streets of Birmingham. With him was another SCLC minister, Ralph Abernathy. They were heading for City Hall, where they would demand change. But they never got there. The police stopped the marchers and arrested Martin. He was led to jail.

He was put in a tiny cell and was not allowed to call anyone. Back home, Coretta was worried and could get no word about him. Then she got a phone call. It was from the president of the United States, John F. Kennedy. He said he would personally look into the matter. Soon after that, Martin was released. He immediately went to work on a new protest. It would later be called the Birmingham Children's Crusade. Hundreds of children marched through the city streets. On the first day, the marches were peaceful. Hundreds of people of all ages were arrested, but there was no violence.

This scene from the King Mural in Washington, D.C., shows Martin leading the bus boycott and in prison.

Firemen hosed demonstrators on the streets of Birmingham.

The next day, however, trouble began. The police chief, Eugene "Bull" Connor, had had enough. Acting on Connor's orders, Birmingham policemen set loose dogs on the marchers. Firemen also sprayed the marchers with firehoses. Connor wanted to stop the protesters once and for all.

But his actions helped the protesters. All around the country, people watched the news and saw what Connor had done. They saw pictures of the Birmingham police dogs attacking children, and they were horrified.

Soon President Kennedy got involved. He appeared on television and announced a new plan. He would propose a new law. If it was passed, segregation in all public places would be illegal.

In Birmingham, the city's leaders finally agreed to Martin Luther King, Jr.'s demands. They would end segregation in the city. It had been a terrible time, but the movement had won.

The March on Washington

Now the civil rights movement was at its peak. Millions of people all across the country understood that change must come. On August 28, 1963, a great demonstration was held in the nation's capital: the March on Washington. Nearly 250,000 people poured into the city. They marched through the streets and headed for the Lincoln Memorial. They were marching for equality.

The huge crowd gathered around the Memorial. The great statue of Abraham Lincoln was before them. One hundred years before, Lincoln had freed the slaves. Now the descendants of slaves, America's black citizens, were demanding true equality.

Martin Luther King, Jr., gave his famous "I Have a Dream" speech to the crowd. In it, he captured the hopes and dreams of millions of Americans, black and white. The moment was one of the high points of the civil rights movement.

Cheers rang out when he finished. People hugged one another and wept for joy. Martin Luther King, Jr.'s dream was wonderful to behold.

Two hundred thousand people gathered at the Lincoln Memorial to hear Martin Luther King, Jr.

The "I Have a Dream" Speech

On August 28, 1963, Martin Luther King, Jr., gave one of the great speeches in American history. Nearly 250,000 people had gathered at the Lincoln Memorial in Washington, D.C. They had come together to demand equal rights for all.

Martin Luther King, Jr., spoke to them and to millions of other people watching on TV. He began reading his prepared speech, but then he stopped and put away his notes. He did not need to read. What he wanted to say was in his heart. All his life he had witnessed racism. Now was his chance to present his vision of equality to the nation and the world.

"I have a dream!" he cried. "I have a dream that one day on the red hills of Georgia, sons of former slaves and sons of former slave owners will be able to sit down together at the table of brotherhood. . . . I have a dream that my four little children will one day live in a nation where they will not be judged by the color of their skin but by the content of their character."

Martin spoke of the faith in the future that everyone must have. "With this faith we will be able to work together, to pray together, to struggle together, to go to jail together, to stand up for freedom together, knowing that we will be free one day. This will be the day when all of God's children will be able to sing with new meaning—'my country 'tis of thee, sweet land of liberty, of thee I sing.' "

The crowd was struck by his words. He said he dreamed that one day there would be freedom for the whole country. And on that day everyone would join hands and sing, "Free at last! Free at last! Thank God Almighty, we're free at last!"

Pain and Honors

Soon, however, it looked as though Martin's dream of peace and justice would never be. A few weeks after the March on Washington, a bomb exploded in a black church in Birmingham. It happened on a Sunday morning, when the church was crowded with people. Four young girls were killed, and many more people were injured.

Some white people did not share Martin's dream of peace and brotherhood. They wanted to keep blacks from getting power, and they were willing to kill to show how serious they were.

Two months after that, and just three months after Martin's hopeful speech, President Kennedy was killed by an assassin's bullet. The nation was filled with sadness. Martin heard the news and knew that there was still great hatred in the nation. He told his wife, ''I don't think I'm going to live to reach forty.''

The year 1963 ended with pain, but Martin continued to lead the struggle for equality. Lyndon Johnson became the new president. He promised to sign the law that President Kennedy had proposed, which would end segregation in public places. Martin kept up the pressure, and President Johnson signed the law the next year. It became known as the Civil Rights Act of 1964. Martin was present at the signing ceremony. It was satisfying to finally see part of his dream become law.

Meanwhile, Martin received many honors for his work. *Time*

magazine named him "Man of the Year." Then, late in 1964, Martin was told that he had won the Nobel Peace Prize, one of the world's highest honors. He and Coretta traveled to Norway, where he was awarded the prize. He was now one of the most loved and respected men in the world.

One Last March

In 1965, Martin led one more march. In Selma, Alabama, as in many other parts of the South, blacks had been stopped from trying to vote. A group of young black activists tried to organize a protest. The police beat the activists to stop them. They even killed one young protester, Jimmie Lee Jackson. Martin came to Selma for Jackson's funeral and saw how bad the situation was. He decided to stage a march from Selma to the state capital, Montgomery, to protest Jackson's death.

Martin led the Selma march.

The first time the marchers set out, state policemen attacked them at the Edmund Pettus Bridge on the eastern edge of Selma, beating them with clubs and firing tear gas at them. TV reports shocked the nation.

Two weeks later, with Martin leading them, the marchers tried again. It was 50 miles from Selma to Montgomery. President Johnson was worried that the marchers would be attacked. He sent the National Guard to protect them. Angry whites stood by the roadside and shouted, ''Niggers go home!'' But no one was injured.

Five days later, the marchers reached Montgomery. They walked past the Dexter Avenue Baptist Church. They marched all the way to the statehouse. There, Martin spoke to a crowd of 25,000 in a voice filled with emotion. He said that everyone wondered how long it would take for segregation to end. ''How long?'' he asked. ''Not long,'' he answered, ''because no lie can live forever.''

The End in Memphis

As the 1960s went on, the United States became involved in a war in Vietnam. Martin Luther King, Jr., believed that this was an unjust war, and he said so. Some people told him he should speak only about the problems of blacks. But Martin answered that he had to speak out. ''I am a citizen of the world,'' he said.

He also was concerned about all the poor people in the United States, both black and white. In 1968, he traveled to Memphis, Tennessee, to march with sanitation workers who were underpaid. Two nights before the march, Martin gave a speech. He seemed in a strange mood. He said that freedom was sure to come, but he also said that he was not sure whether he would be alive to see it.

*Martin with Ralph Abernathy and Jesse Jackson at his hotel
in Memphis. One day later, he would be dead.*

''Like anybody, I would like to live a long life,'' he said. ''But
I'm not concerned about that now. I just want to do God's will. And
He's allowed me to go up to the mountain. And I've looked over.
And I've seen the Promised Land. And I may not get there with you.
But I want you to know tonight that we as a people will get to the
Promised Land.''

The next day, Martin walked out onto the balcony of the motel
where he was staying. A shot rang out, and Martin slumped down.
Ralph Abernathy bent over him and tried to help his friend. But it
was too late. Martin Luther King, Jr., was dead.

The killer was James Earl Ray, a white drifter. He was one of many people filled with anger and confusion in those troubled days. Martin had received many death threats, and there was much hatred in the country. The night before, he had seemed to know that his end was near.

Around the country, people peacefully mourned the fallen leader. But many other people who were confused and frustrated turned to violence. There were riots in many cities. It seemed that Martin's peaceful way might be forgotten.

But it was not forgotten. Since 1986, the United States has officially celebrated Martin Luther King, Jr., Day. Every year on January 15, Martin's birthday, people honor his memory. They remember him as one of the nation's greatest leaders. He was a man who led not with guns, but with words of hope. He was a man who dreamed.

Important Dates in the Life of Martin Luther King, Jr.

1929	Martin is born in Atlanta, Georgia, on January 15.
1951	Martin graduates from Crozer Theological Seminary.
1953	Martin marries Coretta Scott.
1955-56	Martin leads the Montgomery bus boycott.
1957	Martin founds the Southern Christian Leadership Conference.
1962	Martin takes part in protests in Birmingham, Alabama.
1963	Martin delivers the "I Have a Dream" speech at the March on Washington.
1964	Martin receives the Nobel Peace Prize.
1965	Martin leads the Selma-to-Montgomery march.
1968	Martin Luther King, Jr., is shot and killed in Memphis, Tennessee, on April 4.

UNTIL JUSTICE ROLLS DOWN LIKE WATERS
ND RIGHTEOUSN
A MIGHTY STREA
MARTIN LUTHER
11·JUN·1963
ALABAMA GOVERNOR STANDS IN
SCHOOLHOUSE DOOR TO STOP
UNIVERSITY INTEGRATION
MEDGAR EVERS · CIVIL RIGHTS LEAD
ASSASSINATED · JACKSON, MS
28·AUG·1963
250,000 AMERICANS MARCH
WASHINGTON FOR CIVIL RIGH
BAPTIST CHURCH BIR
SCHOOLGIRLS KIL
CAROLE ROBE
ADDIE MAE

Find Out More About Martin Luther King, Jr.

Books: *Extraordinary Black Americans from Colonial to Contemporary Times* by Susan Altman (Chicago: Childrens Press, 1989).

I Have a Dream by Margaret Davidson (New York: Scholastic, 1986).

Gandhi by Nigel Hunter (New York: Franklin Watts, 1987).

The Story of the Montgomery Bus Boycott by R. Conrad Stein (Chicago: Childrens Press, 1986).

Movies: *King: Montgomery to Memphis* is a documentary about Martin Luther King, Jr.'s leadership of the civil rights movement.

Eyes on the Prize is a documentary series that covers the whole civil rights movement.

Places: The Civil Rights Memorial in Montgomery, Alabama, is a tribute to those who died in the struggle for civil rights. It is located in downtown Montgomery, at the corner of Washington and Hull Streets.

The Civil Rights Memorial in Montgomery.

Index